AGNES PRUS

Let it snow

24 RECIPES FOR FESTIVE SWEET TREATS

———

PHOTOGRAPHY BY FRAUKE ANTHOLZ

Hardie Grant

BOOKS

Introduction

Year after year we look forward to Christmas, excitedly awaiting the first snow. As we gaze out of the window, we dream of long winter walks, dancing snowflakes and a white Christmas.

The smell of home-baked, festive treats is a vital component of Advent. If my longing for a walk in the snow gets too much for me, I conjure up the finest snow-covered goods straight from my oven. I dust icing (confectioner's) sugar over bite-sized sweets, encase delicious biscuits (cookies) with dainty coconut flakes and decorate everything with snow-white icing.

From Matcha & Coconut Trees (page 17), to Chocolate & Pecan Snowballs (page 32), Coconut Peaks (page 41) and a Miniature Gingerbread Town (page 44), the recipes in this book will help you to create a genuine winter wonderland in your very own home. For every day in Advent there's a new recipe to help make the dream of a white Christmas come true.

Happy baking with almonds, cinnamon and snow!

Agnes Prus

Mulled Wine Tartlets

MAKES ABOUT 12

FOR THE JAM (JELLY):
125 ML (4 FL OZ/½ CUP) RED WINE
2 STRIPS OF ORANGE PEEL
2 CLOVES
1 CINNAMON STICK
1 PIECE OF STAR ANISE
¼ VANILLA POD (BEAN)
125 ML (4 FL OZ/½ CUP) GRAPE JUICE
75 G (2½ OZ/⅓ CUP) PRESERVING SUGAR 3:1

FOR THE DOUGH:
200 G (7 OZ) BUTTER
140 G (5 OZ/⅔ CUP) RAW CANE SUGAR

SEEDS OF 1 VANILLA POD (BEAN)
PINCH OF SALT
1 EGG
300 G (10½ OZ/SCANT 2½ CUPS) PLAIN
   (ALL-PURPOSE) FLOUR + A LITTLE EXTRA
100 G (3½ OZ/1 CUP) BLANCHED
   GROUND ALMONDS

FOR DECORATING:
ICING (CONFECTIONER'S) SUGAR

EXTRA EQUIPMENT:
STAR-SHAPED COOKIE CUTTERS, IN THREE SIZES

❶ For the jam, put the red wine with the orange peel, spices, scraped out vanilla pod and vanilla seeds into a saucepan. Bring to the boil on a medium heat. Immediately remove from the stove, cover and steep for at least 2 hours. Strain the wine mixture through a sieve and pour back into the pan. Mix in the juice and the preserving sugar. Bring to the boil and fast boil for 3 minutes. Pour into a sterilised jar and allow to set.

❷ For the dough, cream the butter with the sugar, vanilla seeds and salt. Add the egg and beat in well. Add the flour and almonds, and work everything into a smooth dough. Wrap in cling film (plastic wrap) and leave in a cool place for 1 hour.

❸ Roll out the dough to a thickness of 3–4 mm (⅛ in) on a floured work surface, and press out stars in three sizes. Place on baking sheets lined with baking parchment and bake for 10–12 minutes (you might need to take the small ones out of the oven earlier). Remove from the oven and allow to cool on a cooling rack.

❹ Heat the jam in a saucepan and stir until smooth. Spread the jam on the large and medium-sized circles, before stacking them together with the small ones on top. Dust with icing sugar and add a final dab of jam. Store in a tin.

Fruit Bread Swirls

MAKES ABOUT 45

FOR THE FILLING:
7 TBSP HOT WATER
2 TSP CHAI TEA
300 G (10½ OZ/1⅔ CUPS) MIXED DRIED FRUIT
(E.G. FIGS, PRUNES, APRICOTS OR
CRANBERRIES), COARSELY CHOPPED
1 TSP LEMON JUICE

FOR THE DOUGH:
275 G (10 OZ/2¼ CUPS) PLAIN (ALL-PURPOSE)
FLOUR + A LITTLE EXTRA
175 G (6 OZ) COLD BUTTER, DICED

60 G (2 OZ/¼ CUP) RAW CANE SUGAR
2 EGG YOLKS
1 TSP VANILLA EXTRACT
1 TSP GROUND CINNAMON
¼ TSP BAKING POWDER
PINCH OF SALT

FOR THE ICING (FROSTING):
ABOUT 100 G (3½ OZ/GENEROUS ¾ CUP) ICING
(CONFECTIONER'S) SUGAR
ABOUT 3 TSP ORANGE JUICE

❶ For the filling, pour the hot water over the chai tea and steep for 10 minutes. Pour through a sieve. Pulse the dried fruit in a food processor to form a coarse paste. Add the tea and lemon juice, and mix well. Put the filling to one side.

❷ For the dough, quickly knead all the ingredients. On a floured work surface, roll out to a thickness of about 5 mm (¼ in) to form a rectangle (about 20 × 30 cm/8 × 12 in). Roll out the filling between two layers of cling film (plastic wrap) of the same size. Pull off the cling film and carefully lay the filling on the dough. Roll up both layers starting from the long end. Wrap in cling film and chill for about 1 hour in the freezer.

❸ Preheat the oven to 180°C (350°F/gas 4). Unwrap the roll of dough and cut into slices about 8 mm (¼ in) thick. Place the swirls on baking sheets lined with baking parchment and bake for about 12 minutes. Remove from the oven and allow to cool.

❹ For the icing, pour the icing sugar into a small bowl and cream it with the orange juice, if necessary, adding more juice drop by drop until the desired consistency is achieved. Fill into a piping bag with a small opening and decorate the swirls with spirals. Leave until completely dry and store in a tin.

Chocolate Snowmen

MAKES ABOUT 12

FOR THE DOUGH:
250 G (9 OZ/2 CUPS) PLAIN (ALL-PURPOSE) FLOUR
    + A LITTLE EXTRA
50 G (2 OZ/SCANT ½ CUP) COCOA POWDER
PINCH OF SALT
150 G (5 OZ) SOFT BUTTER
130 G (4½ OZ/SCANT ⅔ CUP) SUGAR
75 G (2½ OZ/SCANT ½ CUP) BROWN SUGAR
1 EGG
½ TSP VANILLA EXTRACT

FOR THE ICING (FROSTING):
ABOUT 200 G (7 OZ/SCANT 1⅔ CUPS) ICING
    (CONFECTIONER'S) SUGAR
ABOUT 3 TBSP MILK

FOR DECORATING:
ABOUT 12 CRANBERRIES
2–3 SLICES OF DRIED MANGO

❶ For the dough, mix the flour, cocoa powder and salt together. In a second bowl, beat the butter with the two types of sugar for about 3 minutes until light and creamy. Add the egg and vanilla extract, and stir in for 1 minute. Gradually stir in the flour mixture. Wrap the dough in cling film (plastic wrap) and leave in a cool place for 1 hour.

❷ Preheat the oven to 170°C (340°F/gas 3). Roll out the dough on a floured work surface to a thickness of about 4 mm (¼ in), and press out circles in three sizes (6 cm/2½ in, 5 cm/2 in and 3.5 cm/1½ in). Place the circles, sorted by size, on baking sheets lined with baking parchment. Bake the smallest cookie circles for 6 minutes and the remainder for about 10 minutes. Take out of the oven and allow to cool on a cooling rack.

❸ For the icing, pour the icing sugar into a small bowl and stir with the milk until smooth, if necessary, adding more milk drop by drop until the desired consistency is achieved. Coat the biscuits (cookies) with it, and stack them in descending order of size. Cut the cranberries into small pieces and apply them to the snowmen as eyes, mouths and buttons. Cut the strips of mango into the shape of mini-carrots, and place them on the faces as noses. Leave until completely dry and store in a tin.

Peanut & Oat Cubes

MAKES ABOUT 50

FOR THE DOUGH:
100 G (3½ OZ/1 CUP) WHOLEGRAIN ROLLED OATS
110 G (3½ OZ) MELTED BUTTER
1 EGG
130 G (4½ OZ/⅔ CUP) RAW CANE SUGAR
2 TSP SMOOTH PEANUT BUTTER
1 TBSP GOLDEN SYRUP (OR CORN SYRUP)
¼ TSP VANILLA EXTRACT
LARGE PINCH OF GROUND CINNAMON
PINCH OF SALT

100 G (3½ OZ/SCANT ⅔ CUP) ROASTED UNSALTED
    PEANUTS, CHOPPED
50 G (2 OZ/SCANT ½ CUP) PLAIN (ALL-PURPOSE)
    FLOUR

FOR THE ICING (FROSTING):
ABOUT 150 G (5 OZ) WHITE CHOCOLATE,
    COARSELY CHOPPED
2 TBSP SUGAR, TO TASTE

❶ Preheat the oven to 180°C (350°F/gas 4). For the dough, on a medium heat brown the rolled oats in a pan (without any oil or butter). Pour into a bowl and mix with the butter.

❷ Beat the egg with the sugar until fluffy. Mix in the peanut butter, golden syrup, vanilla extract, cinnamon and salt, then blend in the peanuts and flour. Spread the dough on a 20 cm (8 in) square baking tray lined with baking parchment and bake for about 18 minutes. Take out of the oven and allow to fully cool. Cut into cubes of about 3 cm (1¼ in) using a bread knife.

❸ For the icing, melt the chocolate over a hot water bath (but don't let it get too hot!). Coat one side of each cube with it and allow to cool, then, using a toothpick, decorate patterns on top with the leftover melted chocolate and sprinkle with sugar to taste. Allow the biscuits (cookies) to dry fully overnight, then store in a tin.

5

Matcha & Coconut Trees

MAKES ABOUT 35

FOR THE DOUGH:
50 G (2 OZ/1 CUP) DESICCATED
  (DRIED SHREDDED) COCONUT
60 G (2 OZ/½ CUP) ICING (CONFECTIONER'S) SUGAR
150 G (5 OZ/1¼ CUPS) PLAIN (ALL-PURPOSE) FLOUR
  + A LITTLE EXTRA
2 TSP MATCHA POWDER
125 G (4 OZ) COLD BUTTER, DICED
1 EGG YOLK
GRATED ZEST AND 1 TSP JUICE OF 1 LIME
  PINCH OF SALT

FOR THE ICING (FROSTING):
ABOUT 100 G (3½ OZ/GENEROUS ¾ CUP) ICING
  (CONFECTIONER'S) SUGAR
ABOUT 3 TSP MILK

FOR DECORATING:
GROUND DESICCATED (DRIED SHREDDED) COCONUT

EXTRA EQUIPMENT:
TREE-SHAPED COOKIE CUTTER

❶ For the dough, very finely grind the desiccated coconut with the icing sugar in a coffee grinder or a food processor. Thoroughly mix the flour with the matcha powder and add to the coconut mixture. Add the remaining ingredients and quickly knead everything into a smooth dough. Wrap in cling film (plastic wrap) and leave in a cool place for at least 30 minutes.

❷ Preheat the oven to 160°C (320°F/gas 2). Roll out the dough on a floured work surface to a thickness of about 5 mm (¼ in) and, using the tree-shaped cutter, press out the trees. Place on baking sheets lined with baking parchment and bake for about 15 minutes. To make sure they stay nice and green, the trees should hardly be browned. Take out of the oven and allow to cool.

❸ For the icing, pour the icing sugar into a small bowl and stir with the milk until smooth, if necessary adding milk drop by drop until the desired consistency is achieved. Decorate the biscuits (cookies) with it sparingly and sprinkle with desiccated coconut. Leave until completely dry and store in a tin.

TIP: THE MATCHA POWDER CAN BE REPLACED WITH BARLEY GRASS POWDER.

Apple Gingerbread

MAKES ABOUT 30

FOR THE DOUGH:
70 G (2½ OZ) DRIED APPLE RINGS, FINELY CHOPPED
50 G (2 OZ/SCANT ½ CUP) RAISINS, FINELY CHOPPED
5 TBSP APPLE JUICE
300 G (10½ OZ/SCANT 1 CUP) HONEY
50 G (2 OZ/¼ CUP) BROWN SUGAR
1 TSP BICARBONATE OF SODA (BAKING SODA)
200 G (7 OZ/SCANT 1⅔ CUPS) PLAIN (ALL-PURPOSE)
   FLOUR + A LITTLE EXTRA
120 G (4 OZ/1¼ CUPS) WHOLEMEAL RYE FLOUR
40 G (1½ OZ/¼ CUP) CHOPPED ALMONDS
30 G (1 OZ/GENEROUS ¼ CUP) GROUND ALMONDS
2 TSP GINGERBREAD SPICE MIX
2 TSP GROUND CINNAMON
1 EGG YOLK

FOR THE ICING (FROSTING):
100 G (3½ OZ/GENEROUS ¾ CUP) ICING
   (CONFECTIONER'S) SUGAR
2 TBSP CALVADOS

PLUS:
ABOUT 200 G (7 OZ) PLUM JAM
1 EGG WHITE
DECORATIVE WAFERS

EXTRA EQUIPMENT:
HEART-SHAPED COOKIE CUTTER

❶ For the dough, soak the apple rings and raisins in the apple juice. Warm up the honey and sugar on a low heat (don't boil) until the sugar has melted. Allow to cool until lukewarm and pour into a mixing bowl. Dissolve the bicarbonate of soda in 2 teaspoons water, fold into the flour and add to the honey and sugar.

❷ Mix the rye flour, almonds and spices together. Add the egg to the dough with the rye flour mixture and the soaked dried fruits. Knead everything thoroughly, cover and allow to rest for 2 hours at room temperature.

❸ Preheat the oven to 180°C (350°F/gas 4). Roll out the dough on a floured work surface to a thickness of about 5 mm (¼ in) and press out circles and hearts of about 4 cm (1½ in). Coat half of the circles and hearts in the middle with plum jam and brush them at the edge with egg white, then cover each of them with a second circle or heart. Carefully press the edges together. Place on a baking sheet lined with baking parchment and bake for about 10 minutes.

❹ For the icing, stir the icing sugar with the Calvados until smooth, if necessary adding Calvados drop by drop until the desired consistency is achieved. Take the gingerbread out of the oven, coat with icing while still warm and top with wafers. Allow to dry and store in a tin. Leave for at least 2 days before eating.

Lemon Stars

MAKES ABOUT 25

FOR THE LEMON CURD:
GRATED ZEST AND JUICE OF 1 LEMON
90 G (3 OZ/SCANT ½ CUP) RAW CANE SUGAR
1 EGG
60 G (2 OZ) SOFT BUTTER, DICED
¼ TSP GROUND TURMERIC, TO TASTE

FOR THE DOUGH:
120 G (4 OZ) BUTTER
120 G (4 OZ/GENEROUS ½ CUP) RAW CANE SUGAR
3 EGG YOLKS
1 TSP VANILLA EXTRACT

150 G (5 OZ/1¼ CUPS) PLAIN (ALL-PURPOSE) FLOUR
+ A LITTLE EXTRA
150 G (5 OZ/1½ CUPS) BLANCHED GROUND
ALMONDS
PINCH OF SALT

FOR DECORATING:
ICING (CONFECTIONER'S) SUGAR

EXTRA EQUIPMENT:
STAR-SHAPED COOKIE CUTTER

❶ For the lemon curd, put all the ingredients into a small saucepan and mix well. Warm up on a low heat, stirring constantly, until the mixture thickens. To check whether the curd is ready, dip a wooden spoon in and blow. If a wave-like pattern forms that is reminiscent of a rose, remove the pan from the stove. Whilst the curd is cooling it will further thicken, taking on a spreadable consistency. Fill into a sterilised jar and allow to cool.

❷ For the dough, cream the butter and sugar together. Blend in the egg yolks and the vanilla extract, then add the flour, almonds and salt. Work everything into a smooth dough, wrap in cling film (plastic wrap) and allow to rest in the fridge for 1 hour.

❸ Preheat the oven to 175°C (340°F/gas 3). Roll out the dough on a floured work surface to a thickness of about 4 mm (¼ in) and press out stars, then make a hole in the middle of half of the biscuits (cookies). Place the biscuits on a baking sheet lined with baking parchment and bake for about 10 minutes until golden. Take out of the oven and allow to cool on the baking sheet. Spread lemon curd on the biscuits without a hole, and place a biscuit with a hole on each of them. Dust with icing sugar and store in a tin.

Spiced Cookie Wheels

MAKES ABOUT 40

30 G (1 OZ/SCANT ¼ CUP) BROWN SUGAR
80 G (3 OZ) BUTTER
80 G (3 OZ/⅓ CUP) RAW CANE SUGAR
3 TBSP CREAM
1 EGG YOLK
GRATED ZEST OF ½ LEMON
GRATED ZEST OF ½ ORANGE
180 G (6½ OZ/1⅔ CUPS) PLAIN (ALL-PURPOSE)
    FLOUR + A LITTLE EXTRA
½ TSP GROUND CINNAMON
¼ TSP EACH OF GROUND GINGER, GROUND
    CARDAMOM, GROUND CORIANDER SEEDS AND
    GROUND CLOVES

¼ TSP FRESHLY GRATED NUTMEG
LARGE PINCH OF BICARBONATE OF SODA
    (BAKING SODA)
PINCH OF SALT

PLUS:
ABOUT 80 G (3 OZ/SCANT 1 CUP) FLAKED
    ALMONDS
ABOUT 2 TBSP MILK

EXTRA EQUIPMENT:
    GLASS DISH WITH PATTERN EMBOSSED ON
    THE BASE

❶ Finely grind the brown sugar in a food processor. Put in a bowl with the butter and raw cane sugar and cream the ingredients together. Add the cream, egg yolk, grated lemon zest and grated orange zest and continue mixing for 1 minute. Mix the flour with the spices, bicarbonate of soda and salt, and add to the butter mixture. Work everything into a smooth dough and leave in a cool place for at least 1 hour, wrapped in cling film (plastic wrap).

❷ Preheat the oven to 180°C (350°F/gas 4). Spread the flaked almonds over a baking sheet lined with baking parchment. On a floured surface, roll out the dough in portions to a thickness of about 2 mm (⅛ in). Lightly dust the surface with flour and press patterns into the dough with the base of the glass dish. Cut cookies in the dough using a suitable round cutter and place on the baking sheet scattered with almonds. Remove the remaining flaked almonds from the baking sheet. Brush the biscuits with milk and garnish with flaked almonds as desired. (If the dough has softened whilst being worked, leave the biscuits in a cool place for another 30 minutes before baking.)

❸ Bake for about 10 minutes until golden brown. Take out of the oven, allow to fully cool and store in a tin so they stay nice and crunchy.

Coconut & Almond Sweets

MAKES ABOUT 25

180 G (6½ OZ) WHITE CHOCOLATE, COARSELY CHOPPED
30 G (1 OZ) COCONUT OIL
80 ML (3 FL OZ/⅓ CUP) COCONUT MILK
SEEDS OF ¼ VANILLA POD (BEAN)
GRATED ZEST AND 1 TSP JUICE OF 1 LIME
PINCH OF SALT
ABOUT 25 BLANCHED ALMONDS
60 G (2 OZ/1 CUP) DESSICATED
    (DRIED SHREDDED) COCONUT

FOR DECORATING:
SUGAR STARS

EXTRA EQUIPMENT:
SMALL PAPER CASES

❶ The day before, preheat the oven to 120°C (250°F/gas ½). Put the chocolate and oil in a small ovenproof dish and caramelise in the oven for 60 minutes, stirring well every 15 minutes. Remove from the oven and leave to cool until lukewarm.

❷ Put the coconut milk in a saucepan with the scraped out vanilla pod and the vanilla seeds, bring to the boil and simmer on a low heat for 10 minutes. Remove from the stove, allow to cool slightly and remove the vanilla pod. Pour the milk onto the caramelised chocolate, grated lime zest, lime juice and salt, mix everything together well, cover and leave in a cool place overnight.

❸ The next day, briefly brown the almonds in a pan (without any oil or butter). Press out small portions of dough using a teaspoon, press an almond into each one and shape the mixture into balls between your hands. Immediately roll them in coconut shavings. Place a sugar star on top, and gently press in place. Put the sweets in small paper cases and store in the fridge.

Almond & Apricot Treats

MAKES ABOUT 24

FOR THE DOUGH:
40 G (1½ OZ) BUTTER + A LITTLE EXTRA
45 G (1¾ OZ/⅓ CUP) ICING (CONFECTIONER'S) SUGAR
1 TSP VANILLA EXTRACT
1 EGG YOLK
GRATED ZEST OF ½ ORANGE
100 G (3½ OZ/SCANT 1 CUP) PLAIN (ALL-PURPOSE)
   FLOUR + A LITTLE EXTRA
¼ TSP BAKING POWDER
PINCH OF SALT

2 TBSP APPLE JUICE
½ TSP GROUND CINNAMON
½ TSP VANILLA EXTRACT
20 G (¾ OZ) DRIED APRICOTS, COARSELY CHOPPED
100 G (3½ OZ/SCANT ½ CUP) RAW CANE SUGAR
50 G (2 OZ) BUTTER
2 TBSP HONEY
150 G (5 OZ/1⅔ CUPS) FLAKED ALMONDS
30 G (1 OZ) CRANBERRIES, COARSELY CHOPPED
1 TBSP CANDIED ORANGE PEEL, FINELY CHOPPED

FOR THE COATING:
125 ML (4 FL OZ/½ CUP) CREAM

FOR DECORATING:
50 G (2 OZ) WHITE CHOCOLATE, COARSELY CHOPPED

❶ For the dough, beat the butter with the icing sugar and vanilla extract until creamy. Mix in the egg yolk and orange zest. Mix the flour with the baking powder and salt before adding to the butter mixture. Work into a smooth dough and leave in a cool place for 1 hour, wrapped in cling film (plastic wrap).

❷ Preheat the oven to 200°C (400°F/gas 6). For the coating, mix 1 tablespoon cream with the apple juice, cinnamon and vanilla extract. Add the apricots and steep.

❸ Put the sugar in a saucepan with the butter and honey and caramelise on a medium heat until light brown. Gradually stir in the remaining cream with a wooden spoon. (Take care, as the mixture will foam up and be extremely hot!). Stir in the almonds, cranberries and candied orange peel. Remove from the stove before mixing in the steeped apricots.

❹ Roll out the dough on a floured work surface. Press out circles of about 5 cm (2 in) and place on baking sheets lined with baking parchment. Distribute the almond mixture over them. Bake for 15–20 minutes until golden. Take out of the oven and allow to cool on a cooling rack.

❺ Melt the chocolate over a hot water bath and decorate the biscuits (cookies) with it. Leave to dry and store in a tin.

Lucky Mushrooms

MAKES ABOUT 32

FOR THE DOUGH:
80 G (3 OZ/SCANT ¼ CUP) HONEY
80 ML (3 FL OZ/⅓ CUP) MAPLE SYRUP
40 G (1½ OZ/SCANT ¼ CUP) RAW CANE SUGAR
300 G (10½ OZ/SCANT 2½ CUPS) PLAIN (ALL-PURPOSE) FLOUR
50 G (2 OZ/½ CUP) BLANCHED GROUND ALMONDS
1 TSP VANILLA EXTRACT
½ TSP GROUND CINNAMON
¼ TSP GINGER POWDER
¼ TSP EACH OF GROUND CARDAMOM, CORIANDER SEEDS AND PEPPER
LARGE PINCH OF FRESHLY GRATED NUTMEG
LARGE PINCH OF GROUND CLOVES
LARGE PINCH OF GROUND ALLSPICE
GRATED ZEST OF ½ LEMON
PINCH OF SALT
⅓ TSP BICARBONATE OF SODA (BAKING SODA)
1 EGG, WHISKED

FOR THE ICING (FROSTING):
ABOUT 160 G (5½ OZ/GENEROUS 1¼ CUPS) ICING (CONFECTIONER'S) SUGAR
RED FOOD COLOURING
ABOUT 50 G (2 OZ/⅓ CUP) CHOPPED ALMONDS

❶ For the dough, the day before heat up the honey, maple syrup and sugar in a saucepan at a low temperature, stirring until the sugar has dissolved. Remove from the stove and leave to cool until lukewarm. Mix the flour, almonds, vanilla extract, spices, lemon zest and salt together. Dissolve the bicarbonate of soda in 1 tablespoon water and add to the flour with the whisked egg and the honey mixture. Knead everything into a smooth dough and allow to rest overnight at room temperature.

❷ The next day preheat the oven to 170°C (340°F/gas 3). For the stems, take about 140 g (5 oz) of the dough and roll into a bar 1 cm (½ in) across. Cut into 32 pieces, place on a baking sheet lined with baking parchment and bake for about 8 minutes. Take out of the oven and allow to cool.

❸ For the caps, shape 32 balls (of about 3 cm/1¼ in each) from the remaining dough, place on a baking sheet lined with baking parchment and bake for about 12 minutes. With a sharp knife immediately cut a small hole in the base of each cap and push a stem into it. (The stem should fit tightly, to ensure it will stay in place.) Leave the mushrooms to fully dry.

❹ For the icing, stir the icing sugar with 2½ tablespoons water and a little food colouring until smooth. Brush the mushrooms with it and immediately sprinkle with almonds. Leave until completely dry and store in a tin.

Chocolate & Pecan Snowballs

MAKES ABOUT 60

200 G (7 OZ/SCANT 1⅔ CUPS) PLAIN (ALL-PURPOSE) FLOUR
1 TSP BAKING POWDER
½ TSP GINGERBREAD SPICE MIX
LARGE PINCH OF BICARBONATE OF SODA (BAKING SODA)
PINCH OF SALT
250 G (9 OZ) DARK CHOCOLATE (MIN. 60% COCOA SOLIDS), COARSELY CHOPPED
90 G (3 OZ) BUTTER, DICED
2 EGGS

100 G (3½ OZ/½ CUP) BROWN SUGAR
1 TBSP GOLDEN SYRUP (OR CORN SYRUP)
½ TSP VANILLA EXTRACT
100 ML (3½ FL OZ/SCANT ½ CUP) ESPRESSO
80 G (3 OZ/¾ CUP) PECAN KERNELS, FINELY CHOPPED

FOR DECORATING:
120 G (4 OZ/GENEROUS ½ CUP) SUGAR
100 G (3½ OZ/GENEROUS ¾ CUP) ICING (CONFECTIONER'S) SUGAR

❶ Mix the flour in a bowl with the baking powder, gingerbread spice, bicarbonate of soda and salt, and put to one side.

❷ Melt the chocolate with the butter over a hot water bath.

❸ Put the eggs and the brown sugar in a bowl and beat until the sugar has dissolved. Mix in the melted chocolate mixture and the golden syrup. Add the vanilla extract and espresso and mix in. Add the flour and nuts and briefly blend everything to form a smooth dough. Wrap in cling film (plastic wrap) and leave in the fridge to set, for about 3 hours.

❹ Preheat the oven to 180°C (350°F/gas 4). Pour the sugar and icing sugar separately into two deep dishes.

❺ Press out small portions of dough with a teaspoon and shape into balls. Roll first in the sugar and then in the icing sugar. For a really snowy look, leave the balls in a cool place for 15 minutes then roll in the icing sugar again. Place on baking sheets lined with baking parchment and bake for about 12 minutes. Take the snowballs out of the oven, allow to fully cool and store in tins.

Pearl Sugar Pretzels

MAKES ABOUT 20

3 TBSP HONEY
50 ML (1¾ FL OZ/3 TBSP) GOLDEN SYRUP (OR CORN SYRUP)
2 TBSP MUSCOVADO SUGAR
25 G (1 OZ) BUTTER
150 G (5 OZ/1¼ CUPS) PLAIN (ALL-PURPOSE) FLOUR
20 G (¾ OZ/SCANT ¼ CUP) WHOLEMEAL RYE FLOUR
½ TSP EACH OF ANISEED, GINGER POWDER AND GROUND CINNAMON
LARGE PINCH EACH OF GROUND CARDAMOM, GROUND CORIANDER SEEDS, GROUND CLOVES AND GROUND ALLSPICE

PINCH OF SALT
1 TSP BICARBONATE OF SODA (BAKING SODA)
1 TBSP LUKEWARM MILK
30 G (1 OZ) PEARL SUGAR
GRATED ZEST OF ½ LEMON
1 TBSP CANDIED ORANGE PEEL, FINELY CHOPPED

FOR DECORATING:
PEARL SUGAR
ICING (CONFECTIONER'S) SUGAR

❶ A day in advance heat up the honey, golden syrup, sugar and butter in a small saucepan, and stir until the sugar has dissolved. Leave to cool until lukewarm. Mix both flours, the spices and the salt together in a bowl.

❷ Dissolve the bicarbonate of soda in the milk. Together with the honey mixture, pearl sugar, grated lemon zest and candied orange peel add to the flour and knead everything into a smooth dough. Cover and allow to rest overnight at room temperature.

❸ The next day preheat the oven to 170°C (340°F/gas 3). Divide the dough into about 20 portions, roll them into thin strips and form into small pretzels. Sprinkle with pearl sugar, place on baking trays lined with baking parchment and bake for 8–10 minutes. Take out of the oven, allow to cool and dust with icing sugar. Store the pretzels in tins.

Almond Brittle Snowflakes

MAKES ABOUT 60

FOR THE BRITTLE:
60 G (2 OZ/GENEROUS ⅓ CUP) CHOPPED ALMONDS
60 G (2 OZ/¼ CUP) SUGAR
1 SACHET OF VANILLA EXTRACT

FOR THE DOUGH:
300 G (10½ OZ/SCANT 2½ CUPS) PLAIN
   (ALL-PURPOSE) FLOUR + A LITTLE EXTRA
100 G (3½ OZ) COCONUT BLOSSOM SUGAR
   (ALTERNATIVELY BROWN OR WHOLE CANE SUGAR)
80 G (3 OZ/⅓ CUP) RAW CANE SUGAR
2½ TSP SPECULAAS SPICE MIX, OR MIXED SPICE

PINCH OF SALT
1 EGG
180 G (6½ OZ) SOFT BUTTER

FOR THE ICING (FROSTING):
ABOUT 100 G (3½ OZ/GENEROUS ¾ CUP) ICING
   (CONFECTIONER'S) SUGAR
ABOUT 3 TSP ORANGE JUICE

EXTRA EQUIPMENT:
SNOWFLAKE-SHAPED COOKIE CUTTER

❶ For the brittle, toast the almonds in a pan (without any oil or butter) until they are light brown. Remove them, and on a medium heat caramelise the sugar in a pan with 3 tablespoons water. Stir in the almonds and the vanilla extract. Distribute the mixture over a sheet of baking parchment, allow to cool and crumble.

❷ For the dough, knead all the ingredients into a smooth dough. Add the brittle and knead in. Wrap the dough in cling film (plastic wrap) and allow to rest in the fridge for 1 hour.

❸ Preheat the oven to 180°C (350°F/gas 4). Roll out the dough on a floured work surface to a thickness of about 3 mm (⅛ in), and press out biscuits (cookies) with the snowflake cutter. Place on baking sheets lined with baking parchment and bake for about 10 minutes until crunchy. Take out of the oven and allow to cool on a cooling rack.

❹ For the icing, pour the icing sugar into a small bowl and stir with the orange juice until smooth, if necessary, adding more juice drop by drop until the desired consistency is achieved. Fill into a piping bag with a small opening and decorate the biscuits with a delicate snow crystal pattern (don't use too much, or it will make them too sweet). Leave the biscuits to dry and store in a tin.

Coconut Peaks

MAKES ABOUT 30

FOR THE DOUGH:
65 G (2½ OZ) BUTTER
65 G (2½ OZ/GENEROUS ¼ CUP) RAW CANE SUGAR
1 TSP VANILLA EXTRACT
PINCH OF SALT
2 EGG YOLKS
80 G (3 OZ/⅔ CUP) PLAIN (ALL-PURPOSE) FLOUR
50 G (2 OZ) DARK CHOCOLATE (MIN. 60% COCOA
   SOLIDS), SHAVED

FOR THE COATING:
120 G (4 OZ/2¼ CUPS) COCONUT, DESICCATED
   (DRIED SHREDDED)
2 EGG WHITES

PINCH OF SALT
65 G (2½ OZ/GENEROUS ¼ CUP) RAW CANE SUGAR
1 TSP VANILLA EXTRACT
1 TSP LEMON JUICE
1 TBSP QUARK
1 TSP RUM
1 DROP OF BITTER ALMOND EXTRACT, TO TASTE
1 TSP PLAIN (ALL-PURPOSE) FLOUR

❶ Preheat the oven to 160°C (320°F/gas 2). For the dough, cream the butter, sugar, vanilla extract and salt together for 3 minutes. Add the egg yolks and stir for a further 3 minutes, then blend in the flour. Put the dough in a 20 × 30 cm (8 × 12 in) baking pan lined with baking parchment and spread it out with moistened hands. Bake for about 12 minutes until golden. Take out of the oven and immediately sprinkle with chocolate shavings.

❷ For the coating, on a medium heat brown the coconut shavings in a pan (without any oil or butter). Remove from the pan and allow to cool.

❸ Beat the egg whites with the salt until stiff. Drizzle in the sugar and vanilla extract, whilst stirring. Continue to beat until the mixture is glossy. Stir in the lemon juice, quark, rum and bitter almond extract. Mix the coconut and flour and fold in. Spread the mixture on the dough base. Bake for about 12 minutes, making sure the mixture stays light in colour. Take out of the oven, allow to cool and cut into small triangles with a sharp knife. Store in a tin.

Poppy Seed & Marzipan Hearts

MAKES ABOUT 25

FOR THE DOUGH:
230 G (8 OZ/SCANT 2 CUPS) PLAIN (ALL-PURPOSE)
   FLOUR + A LITTLE EXTRA
150 G (5 OZ) COLD BUTTER, DICED
50 G (2 OZ/SCANT ½ CUP) ICING (CONFECTIONER'S)
   SUGAR
50 G (2 OZ) MARZIPAN, SHAVED
40 G (1½ OZ) WHITE CHOCOLATE, SHAVED
1 TSP VANILLA EXTRACT

FOR THE FILLING:
50 G (2 OZ) GROUND POPPY SEEDS
75 ML (2½ FL OZ/5 TBSP) MILK
2 TBSP RAISINS, FINELY CHOPPED
2 TBSP RAW CANE SUGAR

SEEDS OF ½ A VANILLA POD (BEAN)
GRATED ZEST OF ½ LEMON
PINCH OF GROUND CINNAMON
1 DROP OF ALMOND EXTRACT
1 EGG WHITE

PLUS:
1 EGG YOLK
1 TBSP MILK
ABOUT 50 G (2 OZ/½ CUP) FLAKED ALMONDS FOR
   GARNISHING

EXTRA EQUIPMENT:
HEART-SHAPED COOKIE CUTTER

❶ For the dough, quickly knead all the ingredients and allow to rest in the fridge for about 1 hour, wrapped in cling film (plastic wrap).

❷ For the filling, put the poppy seeds, milk, raisins and sugar in a small saucepan, bring to the boil and simmer on a low heat for about 10 minutes. Remove from the stove, mix in the vanilla seeds, lemon zest, cinnamon and almond extract and leave to cool. Beat the egg white until stiff, then fold in.

❸ Roll out the dough on a floured work surface to a thickness of about 4 mm (¼ in) and press out hearts or circles. Spread 1 teaspoon per biscuit (cookie) of poppy seed mixture on half of the biscuits, leaving the rim uncoated. Slightly moisten the edges. Put a second biscuit on top of each of them. Carefully press together the edges all round, and decorate with the prongs of a fork.

❹ Whisk the egg yolk with the milk and brush the biscuits with it. Garnish with flaked almonds. Bake the biscuits for about 12 minutes until golden. Take out of the oven, leave to fully cool and store in a tin.

Miniature Gingerbread Town

MAKES ABOUT 30

FOR THE DOUGH:
100 G (3½ OZ) BUTTER
100 G (3½ OZ/½ CUP) MUSCOVADO SUGAR
100 ML (3½ FL OZ/SCANT ½ CUP) MAPLE SYRUP
1 TBSP GOLDEN SYRUP (OR CORN SYRUP)
250 G (9 OZ/2 CUPS) PLAIN (ALL-PURPOSE) FLOUR
    + A LITTLE EXTRA
1 TSP GINGER POWDER
1 TSP GROUND CINNAMON
½ TSP FRESHLY GRATED NUTMEG

½ TSP GROUND CLOVES
¼ TSP BICARBONATE OF SODA (BAKING SODA)
PINCH OF SALT
1 EGG, WHISKED

FOR THE ICING (FROSTING):
1 EGG WHITE
150 G (5 OZ/1¼ CUPS) ICING
    (CONFECTIONER'S) SUGAR

❶ For the dough, the day before melt the butter with the sugar, maple syrup and golden syrup in a small saucepan on a low heat, until the sugar has dissolved. Remove from the stove and leave to cool until lukewarm.

❷ Mix the flour, spices, bicarbonate of soda and salt together. Add the sugar mixture and the egg and thoroughly blend everything. Cover and leave to rest in the fridge overnight.

❸ The next day preheat the oven to 160°C (320°F/gas 2). Roll out the dough on a floured work surface to a thickness of 2–3 mm (⅛ in) and press or cut out biscuits (cookies) into the shapes of houses and cars. Place on baking sheets lined with baking parchment and bake for 8–10 minutes. Take out of the oven and leave to fully cool.

❹ For the icing, beat the egg white until stiff. Whilst stirring, sprinkle the icing sugar into it, then stir until smooth. Fill into a piping bag with a small nozzle and decorate the gingerbread shapes with it. To keep fresh, store in a tin.

TIP: TO MAKE THE BISCUITS STAND UP, SIMPLY STICK TWO IDENTICAL SHAPES TOGETHER
WITH JAM OR MARMELADE, MAKING THE BASE BROADER AND MORE STABLE. YOU CAN
ALSO PRESS OUT SMALL RECTANGLES FROM THE DOUGH, BAKE THEM AND STICK THEM
TO THE BACKS OF THE BISCUITS WITH ICING.

18

Pistachio & Raspberry Rings

MAKES ABOUT 20

FOR THE DOUGH:
200 G (7 OZ) BUTTER, DICED
100 G (3½ OZ/SCANT ½ CUP) RAW CANE SUGAR
1 TSP VANILLA EXTRACT
1 EGG
80 G (3 OZ/½ CUP) PISTACHIO KERNELS
220 G (8 OZ/1¾ CUPS) PLAIN (ALL-PURPOSE) FLOUR
  + A LITTLE EXTRA
GRATED ZEST OF 1 LEMON
PINCH OF SALT

FOR THE FILLING:
200 G (7 OZ) RASPBERRY JAM

FOR THE ICING (FROSTING):
100 G (3½ OZ/GENEROUS ¾ CUP) ICING
  (CONFECTIONER'S) SUGAR + A LITTLE EXTRA

FOR DECORATING:
ABOUT 50 G (2 OZ/⅓ CUP) PISTACHIO KERNELS,
  FINELY CHOPPED
25 GOJI BERRIES (OR CRANBERRIES), FINELY
  CHOPPED

❶ For the dough, cream together the butter, sugar and vanilla extract. Add the egg and briefly mix in. Finely grind the pistachios in a food processor and add to the butter mix, along with the remaining ingredients. Knead everything into a smooth dough. Leave in a cool place for about 1 hour, wrapped in cling film (plastic wrap).

❷ Preheat the oven to 175°C (340°F/gas 3). Roll out the dough on a floured work surface to a thickness of about 3 mm (⅛ in). Press out 5 cm (2 in) circles and make a hole in the middle of each one. Place on baking sheets lined with baking parchment and bake for about 10 minutes until golden. Take the biscuits (cookies) out of the oven and allow to cool.

❸ Heat up the raspberry jam in a small saucepan and coat one size of half of the rings with it. Put one uncoated ring on top of each coated one, sandwiching them together.

❹ For the icing, pour the icing sugar into a small bowl and stir 2 tablespoons water into it until smooth. Coat the top sides of the rings with the icing and immediately decorate with pistachios and goji berries. Dust with a hint of icing sugar, leave to dry and store in a tin.

19

Cherry & Poppy Seed Hats

MAKES ABOUT 30

150 G (5 OZ/1¼ CUPS) PLAIN (ALL-PURPOSE) FLOUR
+ A LITTLE EXTRA

50 G (2 OZ/SCANT ½ CUP) ICING (CONFECTIONER'S)
SUGAR

35 G (1¼ OZ/¼ CUP) POPPY SEEDS

25 G (1 OZ/¼ CUP) CORNFLOUR (CORNSTARCH)

125 G (4 OZ) COLD BUTTER, DICED

1 EGG YOLK

½ TSP GRATED LEMON ZEST

PINCH OF SALT

150 G (5 OZ) BLACK CHERRY JAM

PLUS:

1 EGG YOLK, FOR BRUSHING

ABOUT 30 G (1 OZ) WHITE CHOCOLATE, FOR
DECORATING

❶ In a bowl, mix together the flour, icing sugar, poppy seeds and cornflour. Add the butter, egg yolk, grated lemon zest and salt, and work everything into a smooth dough. Wrap in cling film (plastic wrap) and leave in a cool place for 1 hour.

❷ Preheat the oven to 175°C (340°F/gas 3). Pour the syrup off the cherries, drain them and roll them over paper towels until dry. Roll out the dough on a floured work surface and cut into strips about 5.5 cm (2 in) wide. Cut them into equilateral triangles with 7.5 cm (3 in) sides. Put a scant teaspoon of the cherry jam on each dough triangle and gently press the tips together over the jam. (The triangles should not be too big, to avoid the tips slipping during baking.) Place the hats on baking sheets lined with baking parchment.

❸ Whisk the egg yolk with 1 tablespoon water. Brush the hats with it and bake for about 12 minutes. Take out of the oven and leave to fully cool on a cooling rack.

❹ Coarsely chop the chocolate and melt it over a hot water bath. Put a dab on the tip of each hat and allow to set. Leave the hats until completely dry and store in a tin.

Hazelnut & Cinnamon Alphabet Biscuits

MAKES ABOUT 20

150 G (5 OZ/GENEROUS 1 CUP) HAZELNUT KERNELS
100 G (3½ OZ/SCANT ½ CUP) RAW CANE SUGAR
15 G (½ OZ) MARZIPAN, SHAVED
2 EGG WHITES
1 TSP GROUND CINNAMON
PINCH OF SALT

FOR DECORATING:
ICING (CONFECTIONER'S) SUGAR

❶ Preheat the oven to 160°C (320°F/gas 2). Spread the hazelnut kernels out on a baking sheet and roast in the oven for about 10 minutes. Remove, and reduce the oven temperature to 130°C (250°F/gas ½). Wrap the hazelnuts in a tea towel and rub off the skins. Finely chop the cooled nuts in a food processor.

❷ Heat all the ingredients over a hot water bath, stirring until the sugar has melted. Remove from the stove and leave to cool until lukewarm. Fill the mixture into a piping bag with a 1.5 cm (½ in) nozzle and squirt letters onto baking sheets lined with baking parchment. Leave to dry for 15 minutes.

❸ Bake the biscuits (cookies) for 12–15 minutes, jamming a wooden spoon in the oven door for the first 10 minutes so the moisture can escape. Remove and allow to cool.

❹ Dust the cooled biscuits with icing sugar, before storing them in a tin.

TIP: THESE ALSO TASTE DELICIOUS IF YOU DECORATE THEM WITH A COATING OF MELTED MILK CHOCOLATE AND CHOPPED HAZELNUTS.

Walnut Dreams

MAKES ABOUT 40

FOR THE DOUGH:
130 G (4½ OZ/1⅓ CUPS) WALNUT KERNELS
170 G (6 OZ) BUTTER
120 G (4 OZ/GENEROUS ½ CUP) RAW CANE SUGAR
1 TSP VANILLA EXTRACT
1 EGG
1 EGG YOLK
270 G (10 OZ/SCANT 2¼ CUPS) PLAIN
    (ALL-PURPOSE) FLOUR + A LITTLE EXTRA
½ TSP GROUND CINNAMON
LARGE PINCH OF BAKING POWDER
LARGE PINCH OF FRESHLY GRATED NUTMEG
PINCH OF SALT

80 G (3 OZ) DARK CHOCOLATE (MIN. 70% COCOA
    SOLIDS), FINELY CHOPPED
1 TBSP HONEY
LARGE PINCH OF ANISEED

FOR THE COATING:
4 TBSP BROWN SUGAR
2 TBSP HONEY
¼ TSP GROUND CINNAMON

FOR DECORATING:
ABOUT 150 G (5 OZ) WHITE CHOCOLATE, CHOPPED
ABOUT 40 WALNUT HALVES

❶ Preheat the oven to 160°C (320°F/gas 2). For the dough, spread the walnuts out on a baking sheet and roast for about 10 minutes in the oven. Take out and allow to cool. Finely grind 100 g (3½ oz/1 cup) of the nuts in a food processor and finely chop the remainder. Cream the butter, sugar and vanilla extract together. Add the egg and egg yolk and continue to beat for 2 minutes. Mix together the flour, cinnamon, baking powder, nutmeg, salt and ground walnuts and add to the dough. Thoroughly mix in and allow to rest in the fridge for 1 hour.

❷ Take 100 g (3½ oz) of the dough and knead with the chocolate, honey, aniseed and chopped walnuts. Press out about 40 small portions, make balls out of them and leave in a cool place. Roll out the remaining dough on a floured work surface and press out circles of about 4 cm (1½ in). Put a ball on each one and push it into the light-coloured dough. Place on baking sheets lined with baking parchment and bake for about 18 minutes. Remove from the oven and allow to cool.

❸ For the coating, caramelise the sugar and honey in a small saucepan on a medium heat. Mix in the cinnamon. Add the nuts and cover them with the caramel. Spread out on baking parchment and allow to cool.

❹ Melt the chocolate over a hot water bath. Coat the cookies with it, put half a nut on each one and leave the chocolate to dry before storing in a tin.

Orange & Almond Crescents

MAKES ABOUT 65

120 G (4 OZ/1¼ CUPS) BLANCHED GROUND
  ALMONDS
270 G (10 OZ/SCANT 2¼ CUPS) PLAIN
  (ALL-PURPOSE) FLOUR
200 G (7 OZ) BUTTER, DICED
75 G (2½ OZ/GENEROUS ½ CUP) ICING
  (CONFECTIONER'S) SUGAR
2 EGG YOLKS
SEEDS OF 1 VANILLA POD (BEAN)

GRATED ZEST OF 1 ORANGE
PINCH OF SALT

PLUS:
60 G (2 OZ/½ CUP) ICING (CONFECTIONER'S) SUGAR
1½ TSP VANILLA EXTRACT
SEEDS OF 1 VANILLA POD (BEAN)
GRATED ZEST OF 1 ORANGE

❶ On a medium heat, toast the almonds in a pan (without any oil or butter) until they are light brown. Take them out and allow to cool, then put in a bowl with the remaining ingredients and quickly work into a smooth dough. Wrap in cling film (plastic wrap) and leave in a cool place for 1 hour.

❷ Preheat the oven to 175°C (340°F/gas 3). Thoroughly knead the dough. Pull off small portions and shape into crescents. Place on baking sheets lined with baking parchment and bake for about 12 minutes.

❸ Meanwhile mix together the icing sugar, vanilla extract and vanilla seeds and sieve into a deep dish. Mix in the grated orange zest.

❹ Take the crescents out of the oven and leave for a short while to cool. Carefully dip them in the sugar mixture and place on a cooling rack. Leave the crescents to fully cool and store in a tin. Ideally leave them to develop their flavour for a few days before eating.

Crunchy Ginger Shooting Stars

MAKES ABOUT 60

60 G (2 OZ/¼ CUP) RAW CANE SUGAR
25 G (1 OZ) CANDIED GINGER, FINELY CHOPPED
75 G (2½ OZ) BUTTER
1 EGG YOLK
60 G (2 OZ/½ CUP) PLAIN (ALL-PURPOSE) FLOUR
LARGE PINCH OF GROUND CINNAMON
LARGE PINCH OF GROUND CLOVES
LARGE PINCH OF FRESHLY GRATED NUTMEG
60 G (2 OZ/GENEROUS ½ CUP) BREADCRUMBS
60 G (2 OZ/½ CUP) GROUND ALMONDS

GRATED ZEST OF ½ LEMON
½ TSP FRESHLY GRATED GINGER

PLUS:
1 EGG, WHISKED
25 G (1 OZ) CANDIED GINGER, FINELY DICED
ABOUT 3 TBSP SUGAR, FOR SPRINKLING

EXTRA EQUIPMENT:
SHOOTING STAR-SHAPED COOKIE CUTTER

❶ Blend the sugar and candied ginger to a paste in a food processor. Cream with the butter in a bowl. Mix in the egg yolk. Mix together the flour and spices and add to the dough with the remaining ingredients. Knead thoroughly, wrap in cling film (plastic wrap) and leave in a cool place for 1 hour.

❷ Preheat the oven to 170°C (340°F/gas 3). Between two layers of cling film roll out the dough to a thickness of 3-4 mm (⅛ in) and press out shooting stars. Place on baking sheets lined with baking parchment, brush with the whisked egg and decorate with the ginger. Sprinkle with sugar to taste.

❸ Bake for about 10 minutes until golden. Take the stars out of the oven, allow to cool and store in a tin.

Walnut, Fig & Date Moons

MAKES ABOUT 35

FOR THE DOUGH:
100 G (3½ OZ/GENEROUS ¾ CUP) DURUM WHEAT
   FLOUR
90 ML (3½ FL OZ/SCANT ½ CUP) LUKEWARM WATER
100 G (3½ OZ/GENEROUS ¾ CUP) PLAIN
   (ALL-PURPOSE) FLOUR + A LITTLE EXTRA
30 G (1 OZ/¼ CUP) ICING (CONFECTIONER'S) SUGAR
PINCH OF SALT
50 G (2 OZ) MELTED BUTTER

FOR THE FILLING:
60 G (2 OZ/⅔ CUP) WALNUT KERNELS

75 G (2½ OZ/SCANT ½ CUP) MEDJOOL DATES,
   STONED, COARSELY CHOPPED
60 G (2 OZ/⅓ CUP) DRIED FIGS, COARSELY CHOPPED
1 TBSP HONEY
½ TSP GRATED ZEST OF 1 LEMON
¼ TSP GROUND CINNAMON
¼ TSP GROUND CARDAMOM

PLUS:
1½ TBSP SUGAR
½ TSP GROUND CINNAMON
ABOUT 2 TBSP CREAM

❶ For the dough, put the durum wheat flour in a small bowl, pour the luke-warm water over it and allow to swell for 30 minutes. Mix the plain flour in a bowl with the icing sugar and salt. Add the durum wheat flour and butter and blend everything together to form a smooth dough. Wrap in cling film (plastic wrap) and allow to rest at room temperature for 2 hours.

❷ Preheat the oven to 170°C (340°F/gas 3). For the filling, finely grind the walnuts in a food processor. Add all the other ingredients and 1 tablespoon water and blend to a firm paste. Roll it out into a bar 1.5 cm (½ in) across and cut into 3 cm (1¼ in) lengths.

❸ On a lightly floured work surface roll out the dough to a thickness of about 4 mm (¼ in) and press out 5 cm (2 in) circles. Put one length of filling on each circle, enclose with dough and shape into little crescent moons. With the seam facing downwards, place on a baking sheet lined with baking parchment.

❹ Mix the sugar and cinnamon together. Brush the moons with cream and sprinkle with the cinnamon sugar. Bake for about 20 minutes until golden. Take out of the oven, allow to cool and store in a tin.

Index

Even as a child, Agnes Prus filled her parents' kitchen with all kinds of sugary creations at Christmas. She began her career as an art historian, but finally listened to her heart and spent several years learning how to bake in a café in Cologne. When her longing for a white Christmas gets too much, she uses icing sugar, coconut and other snowy treats to conjure the finest winter goods straight out of her oven.

Published in 2019 by Hardie Grant Books, an imprint of Hardie Grant Publishing

Hardie Grant Books (London)
5th & 6th Floors
52–54 Southwark Street
London SE1 1UN

Hardie Grant Books (Melbourne)
Building 1,
658 Church Street
Richmond, Victoria 3121

hardiegrantbooks.com

Original edition © 2017 Hölker Verlag in der Coppenrath Verlag GmbH & Co. KG, Hafenweg 30, 48155 Münster, Germany. Original title: Let it Snow: 24 Plätzchen und Kekse für dich (ISBN 978-3-88117-145-8)

British Library Cataloguing-in-Publication Data.
A catalogue record for this book is available from the British Library.

Let it Snow (ISBN 978-1-78488-255-6)

For the German edition:
  Design: Christiane Heim
  Photographer: Frauke Antholz
  Editor: Franziska Grünewald
  Proofreader: Laura Allenfort
  Typesetter: typocepta, Köln

For the English edition:
  Publishing director: Kate Pollard
  Junior editor: Rebecca Fitzsimons
  Translator: William Sleath

Colour reproduction by p2d
Printed and bound in China by Leo Paper Group